god of missed connections

ELIZABETH BACHINSKY

god of missed connections

ELIZABETH BACHINSKY

NIGHTWOOD EDITIONS

Nightwood Editions
Box 1779
Gibsons, BC Canada V0N 1V0

Design and illustrations by Michelle Winegar
Photograph by Diane Loebl

Nightwood Editions acknowledges financial support of its publishing program
from the Canada Council for the Arts and the Book Publishing Industry
Development Program (BPIDP), and from the British Columbia Arts Council.

LIBRARY AND ARCHIVES CANADA CATALOGUING IN PUBLICATION

Bachinsky, Elizabeth, 1976-
    God of missed connections / Elizabeth Bachinsky.

Poems.
ISBN 13: 978-0-88971-226-3
ISBN 10: 0-88971-226-3

    1. Ukraine--Poetry. I. Title.

PS8603.A33G63 2009   C811'.6   C2009-901268-5

IN MEMORIAM

Morning Star

When every thing is still
and the words we have are changed
before they're wrought, I offer
the way thought thins before
it finds its form, how
across this page the light has changed
and so changes everything.

TABLE OF CONTENTS

1.

2.

3.

My Mother's Red Ukrainian Dance Boots

1.

O, New Moon, Young Prince
Send a man to the radiant North Shore Mountains.
In red clothes you are not to go there.
Take the knives away and approach Elizabeth.
And cut out Satan from the head
And cast him out to the mountains, to the sands, to the waters.
Take Satan from the hair, from under the hair,
From the skin, from under the skin,
From the veins, from under the veins,
And from under the blood.

GODDESS OF SAFE TRAVEL

For Christine Bachinsky

Because the way we got here is thanks to one man. He had a name:
Joseph Oleskiw. I didn't know. Now we do. Because a man can't
grant his own passage, for there is paperwork. Because he led one
hundred thousand people right to where we stand, all of them dead
now, yet we are alive and living in this city. Why bother with history?
Because we can. Because we're curious. Because we want to know.
Because to plough it, you've got to own it. How do you feel about
landowners? Interrogate that thought for a while. Because one day you
can be conscripted into one army and the next day another. Because
extremism thrives. Because you have not lived thirty years and have
many questions. Because these questions may never be answered
in the way you or I might need. Because borders change and it's
confusing. Because there are so many books. Because *because* and we
aren't fucking historians. Still, there is this, and what we do. Sister,
that's not nothing. Because I love you.

GOD OF MECHANICAL ACCIDENTS

*For the children and workers of the Children's Cancer Hospital
Minsk, Belarus*

Make a Church of the Child, how she suffers.
She is two-headed, tow-headed, mythic, cries
for milk with one mouth, succour with the other:
*Where is the seat of the mind, mother? My eyes
are not my eyes. My tongue, not my tongue.*
Her brain a soft peach outside her skull,
how does she live? She has no eyes, this young
Janus, looking forward, looking back.

Outside my window, boxcars stuffed with grain
rattle to the shipyards. Can't see the North
Shore through Vancouver smog—that thin,
brown film over everything. Smell of abattoirs.
August. A woman goes into Chernobyl,
Geiger counter clicking. Photographs miracles.

LETTER TO MY SISTER

Remember that Sunday morning in February?
We went to the Labour Temple in Regina
to watch our cousin Jenny practise
with the Poltava dancers. The family had
buried our grandmother's ashes the day before
beside our grandfather's grave in a graveyard
just outside the city. It was bitter cold.
It was snowing. Everyone wore long black coats.
Our mother and aunts and uncle lowered
Grandma's urn into a hole in permafrost
so hard the gravedigger must have had to drill it
with an auger. Next day, we watched
Jenny dance. I remembered Jenny from
years ago at our cousin Dale's wedding outside
Medicine Hat; that same wedding where Mom
had a low blood sugar late at night and almost
died because we couldn't find any juice or
Life Savers in the hotel room. We'd danced
all night in our polka-dot dresses, begged
Jenny to spin in the middle of the dance floor
all ba-donk-a-donk-donk and junk-in-the-trunk,
but she refused and refused until, finally, she gave

up and spun like a revved-up ballerina.
It was awesome, years later, to see her dancing
at the hall with the whole troupe. They were so
young, weren't they? Warming up, the girls
seemed like ballet dancers in their legwarmers
and leggings and the boys were lean and tall
and wore soccer jerseys. Man, those boys could jump.
They'd swagger from one end of the hall
to the other and mimic dance moves they'd studied
on a video sent from Ukraine. They were stars.
And the girls; you could tell those girls loved them.
No wonder Jenny didn't want to take the stage
at that wedding. That job's for men. But she could
spin and spin and spin and spin. Across town,
Granny's ashes lay newly marked by a numbered
flag flying from a four-foot pole in case
we should need to find her in the snow. Jenny told us
she'd found our mother's red boots in the attic
at the hall. Her name *Cathy Gnius* marked on the soles
in black marker. I mean, I know we know the story
of how our parents met, but didn't you think
it felt like proof, knowing those boots were there?

Where radiation plumbs the earth and saturates the foliage
surrounding Chernobyl. Where one may purchase a doll
in the shape of the Führer. Where a woman is prime
minister, her president poisoned. Whose dancers are paid
and so dancers are excellent. Whose capital is cosmo-
politan as any in Europe. Where pornography is a popular
career. Where one can get an AK-47 and hire a pretty girl
to shoot it. Where irradiated wolves populate abandoned cities.
Where Poles say Lvov; Ukrainians, Lviv. Where archaeologists
discover pyramids and citizens unearth Roman coins from
their gardens. Where ruins are a matter of course. Where
construction workers built a sarcophagus around Reactor 4.
Where babies are born with deformities like those
seen later in Iraq. Whose borders are shared with Russia,
Belarus, Poland and Moldova. Where 'oblast' means 'province.'
Where the Dnieper Hydroelectric Station "continues to fuel
the adjacent industrial complexes with an output of 3.64 billion
kW an hour." Where the Verkhovna Rada recognized Holodomor
as genocide in 2006. Whose population of people living
with HIV/AIDS is the highest in Europe. Whose young poets
recite to throngs in public parks. Whose Orange Revolution
was televised in the West.

ON THE DAY WE WERE MARRIED

After Sergei Parajanov

The elder men led you to the church
and left you blindfolded at the door.

Inside, I was also blindfolded. Inside,
the women waited to lead you to me.

I stood in the pavilion in a long white gown
and red woollen stockings.

All I could grasp was the singing,
then I felt you at my side, then

the yoke. We were harnessed to one another
like creatures from the field.

You, husband, slipped your shoulders free.
I could sense you before me.

The air stirred about us.
I knew we were alone.

EVOLUTION OF THE SPECIES

In Belarus, it's said, men fear
to make love with their women.
Who can take the chance
to take to bed such lovers?
Since Chernobyl, children
arrive in fabulous shapes,
legs and arms on backwards.
Some are born without eyes.
1986: the little mothers
pulled carrots from their gardens,
unconscionably lush
and tasty.

GODDESS OF HEALTHY CHILDREN

For Neela Emiliana Rader (b. 2005) on her sixteenth birthday

In a dream I had of you before you were born,
I birthed you to steel drum-and-Casiotone
on a cluttered balcony above Commer-
cial Drive: Vancouver, 2005. Your mother
named you Addy (as in Adelaide) which, in
my state, seemed right enough. You had a twin—
a boy who never got a name. How strange.
When you came, you were neither boy nor Adelaide.

At the time of this writing, your eyes still had no hue.
What colour are they now… are they grey? What do
you see from your window, whom do you love?
Look at your hands. They are your hands. They move
through space as fish slip through a stream.
What tastes please your tongue, what do you dream?

AN UPROOTED TREE

Surma, Cossack bugle, carved from birch.

Trembita, signal giver, wrapped in birch.

Husla, strung plank, carved from birch.

Tsymbaly, struck with sticks, carved from birch.

SEVEN SHOT RABBITS

Seven shot rabbits lie on concrete, face down on concrete.

Now they must be cleaned. There is only the passive construction.

The rabbits' fur is soft and brown. They lie face down. Shot through

their heads, their blood only moves when their heads are moved.

They have soft, red-dipped ears. You grab one there and lift it.

It drips and, quick, you pull its fur away—an easy act, to undress a rabbit.

In a moment, you will skin the others. But, for now, they are still rabbits.

It was 1933. Twenty-five thousand kulaks a day
were starving in the streets of Eastern Ukraine
and children had begun to go missing. In a market
in Poltava, meat appeared where none had been
before. Mothers forbade their little ones to leave
the house. But they perished so quickly, some
slew their weakest and fed the flesh to other,
stronger, children. Better to serve your own
than have them hunted in the streets and sold
in place of bread.

HOLODOMOR

Seven years. Fuck you, paper or plastic.
I see some girl come through the doors.
We went to high school together.
I don't want to see her
seeing me in my smock. Is this a smock?
I don't care. I stock the milk.
I hate working at the supermarket.
I hate the people. All of them buying stuff
they're going to eat. I'm never hungry.
I make some money, I go home.
I like to drink. I don't care what you think.
Last week the manager sent out an email
that said get happy or go home, more or less.
Did he mean me? What if I just went home?
On a hot day, I stand in the backroom
in the fridge where it's really cold,
where the butchers keep the beef
and the chicken.

GODDESS OF REPETITION

This season I can't eat fish in any form.
I have friends, conservationists, who claim to love
the spawn smell: like semen, like sulphur, like corpse-
from-the-grave-knotted-fist-punched-up-through-
soil. The fist flies open. The fingers writhe
with flies. Sashimi's out. The flesh feels wrong
on my tongue. I keep seeing eyes, thousands of eyes
blown open, picked out on the rocks. Gulls wing
their white bodies through leaves by the shore.
Those birds only leave bones.

What is it my friends love? The smell or the sentiment?
Here, in my yard: basic phenomenology. What was lost,
returns. I go down to the rocks and stare and stare.
Clutch a scarf to my mouth when I get too near.
I am impressed by how quickly the bodies decompose, whole
corpses turn to undulant translucent jelly.
I can neither love the smell nor turn away.

And now all the neighbourhood students are drinking
expensive-ish beer on their balconies thinking of the javelin
toss love can be (at any age, but especially) when you're
young and wearing carefully purchased footwear and
accessories. One girl thinks one day I won't remember this
balcony, like tomorrow, while another's sure she's met
her future husband, an MBA from San Francisco and dear
god what's he doing in Canada what a boon for the dating
community (he's straight I mean thank *god*...) while the next-
door neighbours lie in bed and wonder if it isn't time
to move out to the suburbs, maybe get a chunk of property,
have a kid. Trade one noise for another.

It's not that living in a city seems superfluous when you're
in it, but only that it's superfluous when you are out of it
and conversation's lacking everywhere in the end. Consider
this cluster of stargazer lilies. Seven blossoms for two dollars
at a Chinese grocery, but their perfume's too heady for such
a small room. It's four a.m. and the clubs are turning out
the young. Shame to put the blossoms on the balcony.

Hair off your face for starters. Red.
Bright red lipstick. Something that will read
from a distance. Don't worry about your eyes.
Chances are, people won't see them.
What's campy? Wear something bright.
The polka dots will do. For the shoes?
That depends on what you want. If you want
people to look at your feet, wear red.
If you want people to look at your face,
wear navy. Go with the red. On stage, wear
a huge smile at all times. You must project
electric animation. No glazed eyes. Perform
to individuals in the crowd, never to the whole
swarm. Never treat them like a lump.
Don't pan the crowd. Take time to connect.
You are a performer. You belong here.

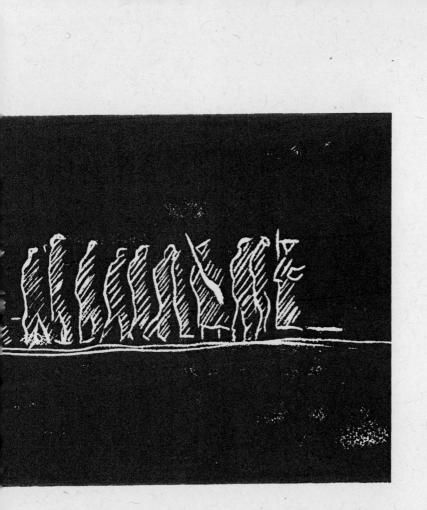

Men Walking, Castle Mountain Internment Camp, Banff, 1917

2.

What a lot people knew and what a lot they've forgotten.
They've forgotten as much as they've learned.
And how much they have forgotten in vain!

–Andrei Bitov, *A Captive of the Caucasus*

> And the soothsayer prophesied.
> Charming the evil eye,
> For three coins,
> Pouring destiny and fortune from the wax.
> —Taras Shevchenko

2005. A woman, twenty-nine. Dark hair pulled back into a ponytail. Ankles crossed beneath her desk. She sits in a rented room before a small white laptop computer. She types,

1911. Michael Bazynski [*sic*] sits, seasick, in the hold of a ship that sailed from Odessa. Though he believes he will be welcomed in his new country, he will not be surprised to learn that he is mistaken. He won't have enough money to get home.

Come out of hiding, baba, she says. Teach me to pour the wax.

What does she see from her window? Apartment buildings. Hastings Street. She takes a book from her desk and reads,

> A little dose of them may even in variation, do good, like a minute dose of poison in medicine… I am not saying we should absolutely shut out and debar the European foreigner as we should and do the Oriental. But we should in no way facilitate his coming.
> –Stephen Leacock, 1930.

You are all of this Pain and Suffering.
Prickly and sore,
I enjoin and summon you,
From the head, from under the head.
From the crown of the head,
From under the crown of the head,

On some construction sites, she writes, there is a big machine that construction workers use to separate different-sized stones. When I was a kid, I played with a small plastic version of this same machine. Tip the toy in one direction and all the different-sized marbles fall into a reservoir. Tip it in the other direction and only the smallest marbles make it through. Many get sifted out. A radio has switched on in a distant room. It whispers the news, traffic patterns, advertisements for hamburgers. The radio competes with Lars von Trier's *The Five Obstructions* playing on the DVD player in the living room. Both sounds are in the background. This page is the foreground.

1911. Paris, France. Stephen Leacock sips eau de vie. At 27 Rue de Fleurus, Gertrude makes love to Alice. Tomorrow the women would like to buy paintings. "Remember," Gertrude says. "We never hid. We moved to Paris."

"Yes, Love," says Alice. "We did that."

1914. Winnipeg, Canada: Michael Baczynski boards a train bound for Banff, Alberta, where there is a labour camp in the Rockies. He will live there six years.

How does the girl work? Like this.

Soldiers put Michael on a train bound for a work camp in the Rockies with sixteen other young men. Some, Michael knew from AUUC meetings at the Labour Temple in Winnipeg, others he did not. West of Calgary, he saw his first mountains. Dizzying, rising black-green from roiling lapis-coloured water. The forests so dense it was impossible to discern the land beneath them. And then the land finally did appear, a white swath of ice curving upward like the bottom of a terrible basin.

From the eyes, from under the eyes,
From the nose, from under the nose,
From the mouth, from under the mouth,

The prisoners cut two-by-two-foot blocks of ice from the Bow River and loaded them, dripping, onto low flat wagons. Half a million blocks in all—and all the while, that strange pale green Bow water sluiced below the surface of the ice. That same water the men watched funnel past the quarries all summer as they cut stone from Tunnel Mountain for the hotel across the valley. Days heaped upon them.

Monday, January 29, 1917.

Fine, cloudy, very cold—some snow. Temperature, –11° Max. and –20° Min. No prisoners of war out on park work a.m. or p.m.—too cold.

Tuesday, January 30, 1917.

Fine, cloudy, very, very cold. Temperature, –30° Max. and –36° Min. No prisoners of war out on park work due to extreme cold weather in a.m.

Wednesday, January 31.

Fine, cloudy, extremely cold. Temperature –25° Max. and –43° Min. No prisoners of war out on park work in a.m. In p.m. 20 prisoners of war escorted by 25 troops worked at toboggan slide from 2 p.m. to 4:30 p.m. Extremely cold with raw east wind.

As the morning progresses, the girl becomes concerned with breathing, eating, fucking, shitting. What is she thinking about? Downstairs, her Chinese-speaking neighbours are smoking. So, there is a downstairs. She can smell the neighbours' smoke. Their smoke makes her aware of them, and a little annoyed. When it is time to use the kitchen, she is careful not to run the microwave and the kettle at the same time for fear of tripping the breaker. If she trips the breaker, she will have to go downstairs and ask the neighbours to flip it. They may not understand her. She types,

I have some money.

I have my own money?

> *From the neck, from under the neck,*
> *From the ears, from the hearing,*
> *From the nape, from under the nape,*

1933. Eastern Ukraine. A Party official writes,

I saw people dying in solitude by slow degree, dying hideously, without the excuse of sacrifice for a cause. They had been trapped and left to starve, each in his home, by a political decision made in a far-off capital around conference and banquet tables.

1934. Alberta. A farmer clears land that won't yield for fifteen years. A police officer leans nearby, watches, gnaws the end of a carrot he pulled from a garden at the side of the house. What about deportation, he says. Don't you care about being made to leave?

You see how my kids are dressed, the farmer replies. You see what furniture we have, what food we eat. Do you think it is possible for life to be any worse?

No, says the policeman.

2007. British Columbia.
She eats.

1932–1933. Holodomor.

She can't begin to write
about this.

How to repress a memory

1: The event must be proven to be true.

2: The persons to whom the event occurred must not speak
of the event for many years.

Write one true thing, then another.

> *From the shoulders, from under the shoulders,*
> *From the chest, from under the chest*
> *From the viscera, from under the viscera,*

"These Are Your Parks," said the park brochure. "Come and Enjoy Them."

In the Danish film, Jørgen Leth's perfect woman speaks perfect French, is blonde-haired and blue-eyed smokes, suicidally, inside an expensive-looking car. In the film, she uses a bidet.

She can't begin to write. What then?

She types,

O. I am making love. My husband's hands are on either side of my body. He lies behind me on our bed and enters me. He holds his cock still inside me. He reaches around and holds my breasts in either hand. I twist so that my back is flat on the bed, while my hips remain turned. In this position, my husband can kiss my breasts while still fucking me from behind. Now, his mouth is very close to my ear. He whispers to me, kisses my neck, my ears, my eyes. In this position, I am able to close my legs tightly around him. The sound of my husband's voice is effective. Now, it is effective. He has asked me if I might come. I do.

Rich folks have complicated ways of dealing with their shit. Three-ply toilet paper. Bidets. All those rich assholes perched over the cleanest porcelain.

From the guts, from under the guts,
From seventy joints
From the lower back, from under the lower back,

Memory Fact Parenthesis

The actual

What they called their policies

What their policies were

Another thing I am interested in is

I wonder why

A question I have is

Why must I write about my lovemaking?

So that I might remember it.

As for the Galacians I have not met a single person in the whole of the Northwest who is sympathetic towards them. They are from the point of view of civilization, ten times lower than the Indians.

–Father Morin, *Alberta Tribune*, February 4, 1899

Im(migrant).

No. Not the present tense.

My name. Here,

....

From the thighs, from under the thighs,
From the knees, from under the knees
From the calves, from under the calves,

Thursday, February 1, 1917.

Fine, cloudy, extremely cold—worst yet but signs of changing. Temperature –3° Max. and –50° Min. No prisoners of war out on park work in a.m. except 24 for Ice Palace and 40 for toboggan slide who left camp at 10:40 a.m. In p.m. temperature moderated and gangs were out at Recreation Park, Cave and Basin Rd.

Saturday, February 3, 1917

Early a.m.—very mild—dull, cloudy at 9 a.m. 24° above, at 11 a.m. 14° below. Started snowing from east at 10:30 a.m.

154 prisoners of war out on park work. Lieutenant Davis left for noon on duty to Calgary. No work by prisoners of war in p.m. Tickets were given out to prisoners of war in p.m. about 20 refused to sign payroll.

alone.　　alone.　　alone.

Michael took a knife and carved a hole in his gut, but he didn't die. He crawled beneath his bunk and slit his neck. *These men will end us. The barracks, the wire, the white mountains. All dead. All dead.*

These are your Vermilion Lakes, Michael. Open them. And, oh, yes, his blood drained from him in the dark. When soldiers found him drowning, not

one said, *Oh, but he is dead, he is dead.*

> *From the ankles, from under the ankles*
> *From the middle of the feet, from under the middle of the feet,*
> *From the toes, from under the toes,*

Internment camps, 1914–1920

Halifax
Quebec
Montreal
Toronto
Kingston
Petewawa
Spirit Lake
Kapuskasing
Brandon
Lethbridge
Vernon
Nanaimo
Port Arthur
Amherst

Among the interned:

Ukrainians (Ruthenians, Galacians)
Poles
Germans
Hungarians
Romanians
conscientious objectors
Some women
Some children
Mostly men

She types,

In my family, we don't speak of family.
And we don't speak of the past.

What is there to know? I'm not afraid to ask.

> Canadians were afraid not only that this imported proletariat could not be assimilated, but also that it would drag down Western society and destroy the British character of the country.
> —Jaroslav Petryshyn, 1985

From the soles, from under the soles.
Go there beyond the range of dogs' barking,
Beyond cocks' crowing, where people do not go,
Where church services are not conducted!
I give you a hen with chicks, a cat with kittens
A sow with piglets, a duck with ducklings, a goose
with goslings.

The morning is finished.

Bars of light slant through the blinds.

She types,

Look up: Proletariat

Go away, take them with you, and carry them with you
To the blue seas, to deep streams.
There you will sift through sand, bathe in water,
Wrap yourself in a leaf!
Swing on a branch.

The Sarcophagus, Chernobyl, Ukraine

3.

Take Satan, Send Him to the Mountains
To the sands, to the waters, and let Elizabeth alone.
Take Satan from the skull, from under the skull,
And from the brain,
And from the forehead, from under the forehead,
And from the brows,
And from the eyes, from under the eyes,
And from the face,
And from the nose, from under the nose,
And from the lips,
And from the teeth, from under the teeth,
And from the tongue
And from the throat, from under the throat,
And from the blood.
Take Satan
And send him to the mountains, to the sands, to the sea, to the waters.
Let her alone like the Mother brought the Lord God into the world.
And cleanse her from the devil.

GODDESS OF INCONGRUITY

All our lives we've known the atomic bomb
but that's okay, we've got these sedans.

Someday, we'll all be middle class!

Get thee to Holt Renfrew.
Get thee to Lviv.
Get thee to thy toilet brush.
Get thee to thy condominium smack dab in a downtown core.

You tired? I'm tired.
Bitch, please.
Got to find time to fix my ship. I sail in a hour.

Oh Jesus, here it comes again.
That weird nausea… *thing*.

I have indefinable dust in my eye.

If you can't trust your digital cable,
what can you?

'86

I was ten years old the year Chernobyl burned,
the very same year that Expo '86
came to Vancouver and the city changed forever.
For I will always think of China, the China pavilion
to be exact, each time these years later I pass
the China Gate at Dr. Sun Yat-Sen's Classical
Chinese Gardens. We were moving then, all of us,
from one place to another. Now, I'm haunted
by the SkyTrain doors' perfect open fifth
then that smooth electronic contralto programmed
to reassure one rides the *Expo Line to Waterfront
Station.* That line stretches out behind us: concrete
contrails left over from '86. Eighty-six,
the year Chernobyl burned hot as the centre
of the earth, the sun, and men hurried in.

GODDESS OF ANTHROPOMORPHISM

Tonight the forest is lit by a full-faced moon.
We sleep with the curtains open. Black water
winks past the riverbank through the trees.
We were from the city. And now we are from
the country, too. In the spring, teenagers
will appear with their titanium fishing rods
and in the summer, they will ride rubber inner-
tubes downstream. Masses of flesh
will chirp and yip on the whitewater where,
not ten months before, the whole place reeked
of chum. Chip bags and beer bottles and cell-
phones in hand, parents will prop plastic chairs
in the shallows and eat takeout burgers
while their little ones paddle out in the pools.
The river is a silent rush of rivergrass
and the stream goes about its decomposition.

My husband's hands are slippery on my thighs.
He can't help it, he says *We are two slick fish…*
and floodlights illuminate our gravel driveway.
We sit up, caught, momentarily, in our own

harsh light. One minute, two, and the flood clicks
off again. I can hear the refrigerator keeping
things cold in the kitchen, rooms away. What
is out there? What creature slouches through
the yard so late at night? *Anthropomorphism,*
I say, *is a dangerous business.*

If the mind is a vast and empty plain of stone,
nothing sticks, nothing stays. The floor's worn
down (as if such stone could wear). There's more
where that came from, friend. More nothing. No,

the metaphor's all wrong. The mind is smooth
as split obsidian. Look in. The glass is black,
it won't look back. It's a thing, neither human,
nor animal, nor the two entwined. No twilit bulk

to skulk the uninterrupted horizon. Others
populate their poems with things, look to their lives
as evidence: to what do I owe, to whom? We look
on this geology. It shrinks back through the trees.

INT. BACK OF POLICE CAR.
NIGHT OR NOTES FOR A FILM IN
WHICH AN INTERNATIONAL PEDOPHILE
RETURNS TO CANADA TO AWAIT TRIAL
AND CERTAIN IMPRISONMENT

Close on a man's face in shadow pressed
to a rain-slicked window. Nighttime cars rush past,
illuminate his orange jumpsuit. What has he done?

The time goes by like this: They are teenagers.
They are in their thirties. They are teenagers.
They are in their thirties. They are in their thirties.

Ensemble cast. Eleven protagonists.
Jennifer says to Jonathan, I don't know you,
I only know the place we met. Where's Steven?

Where's Laura? Where's Sasha? Where's
Amber? Where's Mercedes? Where's Sara?
Where's Dave? Where's Tina? Where's Matt?

GODDESS OF CHANCE ENCOUNTERS

A woman finds a jawbone at the beach, kicks
what she thinks is a seal skull in the sand. Up comes

a human bone—the lower half of the face, but for the flesh.
She puts it in a bag and gives it to some police

on Denman Street. She receives a peculiar look.
Homicide grills her for an hour, makes her show

the place it washed ashore. She goes home without
the bone, but wants to know whom she found.

How long did that jawbone roll before the ocean
punished it to shore, the storm that brought it freak

enough to knock out the city's power and bring a half-built
building down on a parking lot of limousines;

seven stories of steel construction fallen
to the ground; English Bay boiling with bones even a jogger

can find in the chop? The woman, who'd left her husband
not long before, told me she felt outside herself, fallen

for a man she met in passing at a party where
they didn't touch, didn't speak, but they knew, and everything

changed in the space of a week. Poor thing. She can't stop
thinking of the teeth. Whose they were,

whose they weren't. She sees herself, of course,
but also someone else. Someone she doesn't know at all.

CELEBRATION

Cancer's what gets us. Got Grandpa. Got Baba.
It turns you yellow at the end. So, I've been smoking
again. Stupid, right? By why not. I keep thinking how,
in the Arctic, in the eighties, it's said Russians sunk nuclear subs
below the ice and now it's too expensive to recover them.
Now radiation's working its way along the North Pacific
Gyre and eventually the ocean will be full of the stuff.
That's what oceans get for being so efficient. Stupid oceans.
We're in a new century now and American soldiers have
been bombing Iraq with depleted uranium weaponry.
Health effects can range from "fatigue and muscular pain
to genetic disorder, chromosome aberrations, and
malignancies," which present themselves in children,
just like they have in Chernobyl. What are kids supposed
to do when a reactor melts down and they aren't even born yet?
When I was a kid, David Suzuki produced *The Nature of Things*.
Remember that show? He used to say, *If we start now, we can change things.*
That was in the eighties. He's not saying that now. Now,
he says we ought to scream. You know what makes me
scream? The small-bodied creatures of the oceans. How
they're busy swallowing the tiny plastic beads in your Oil

of Olay Purifying Body Wash with Sea Salts and Microbeads
till they're choked with nurdles. But they make
your skin so smooth! Someone once sang, *We're lovers*
in a dangerous time. I think he was talking about AIDS.
Have I got this right? How can I know? Can't
we have a drink or go to Paris or work out at the gym?
If I toast you, let's pretend it's in celebration.

AT CASTLE MOUNTAIN

Eighty years since wooden buildings stood
among these pines and what is left? Soft
impressions in the forest floor. The earth
falls in upon itself and swallows wood—
but what is this? My friend with whom I've come
has sharper eyes than me. He sees the copse
as ghostlike, plucks a tin from the rocks
and bends to pull a bucket from the loam.

Who could tell this mountain is a tomb
from which no man could flee and hope to live.
Aren't we small; who could tell we've stood here?
Pace it out, Sam Pane. Help me walk some
paces around the camp. It was here they lived.
Can you make out the perimeter? The wire?

From where she was standing she could see
the boys were watching her and had been watching her
for most of the night it seemed as if there were a secret
between them which she attributed to the fact they were
boys she felt especially lovely in her polka-dotted
skirt and socks and had been sad for four days since
her father had left home to discover his personal financial
power with an even lovelier telemarketer from Winnipeg.
    Such a Lonely!
One boy put a hand on her leg; one boy put his hand
in her hair; one boy kissed her mouth; one boy kissed
her neck; one boy put his hand inside her blouse;
one boy kissed her ear; one boy smoothed her sweater;
one boy pulled her ribbon; one boy rocked her
in his arms, one boy lifted her; one boy pulled her
mouth; one boy opened her. What a lark! Twenty
cocks shuttling under the white spot so white it was like
blinding white light as twenty tongues and two hundred
fingers found their pleasure at once she woke beneath the goal
posts. She could feel the close-clipped lawn was cool
beneath her cheek.

BROTHER, MY BROTHER,
LET'S SEE WHAT YOU GOT

What's the status with Ralph? Do we still like him
now that he lives in a doorway?

Where will we go for dinner? What are those women
going on about? *Meh meh meh… We don't have enough*

public sex. If only I had a backyard… O god. Today
is pedophilic. That man will travel to Thailand.

That man will pay for brown boys. Unspeakable
acts all around us. What is it? It is the Number Four.

You are never alone. Get it straight. Now that you
are famous, someone will always spot you.

Specifically. Specifically in the moment when you drop
your wallet or stand up and say, *Don't touch me.*

Speak to no one. Now is not the time for pleasantries.
Read the magazine. Read the advertisements for colleges

and universities and upgrading and schools which specialize
in English as a second language even if it's your fourth.

There's the woman with the brownish-red burns on her face,
half her hair given to fire. That man is drunk. That man is

drunk and pissing on his seat. That man is drunk and standing
in the alcove and pissing up a wall. That man is shouting

at pedestrians. There is the roadwork. There is the pit
in the ground. There are the trendy stores. Categorize

your body in this way: which kind of pornography suits it
best? Spit your gum with such force it sticks to that BMW.

No, that top in the window will not fit you. Such tits!
No tits? Then brother, my brother, let's see what you got.

HEARSAY IN THE VALLEY
OF CONDOMINIUMS

I am writing to tell you: that story
I'd overheard about those pygmy

remains? It ran as a practical joke on
the part of city planners or some

local newspaper flunky; I'm not
sure which. Bridge construction went

ahead as planned.
There were, and are, no pygmies on that land.

And, furthermore, that kids' water
park town council tore

down to replace with a yuppie gas station,
is not a gas station.

It is an improved playground.
I got confused when they tore the old

stuff out. For a while, it looked like they
were building a gas station. They

weren't. This "new" water park is, apparently,
more environmentally sound. Which is not to say

that yuppies aren't moving into the area
in droves, because they are.

And the new mayor,
who is also a gangster,

plans to turn his offices into
a Starship Bingo.

GOD OF UNFULFILLED LONGINGS

> Happiness where are you? I haven't got a clue.
> —Eytan Mirsky

Gina—pretty, thirty-two, and who wears a lot of black, not
because she is in mourning but because she's got nothing
else to wear—has started making love with a boy of nineteen
on a semi-regular basis, a practice she finds vastly rewarding
although occasionally problematic, which is not to say the boy
hasn't demonstrated a remarkable learning curve.

Elephants, having been hunted into near extinction, paint!
Sometimes better than people!

This one time, Gina's boy (trapped in an elevator) thought:
I'm trapped in an elevator. You hear stories like this and never believe them.
The elevator rose thirty-six floors at an astonishing speed before
he hit the emergency button which, to his surprise brought him
obediently, politely, to the ground floor, and he walked right out.

YOUNG FAGGOTS

Elizabeth, the day is near
when you will regret all those years
you sat on your ass
complaining of lack
or of beauty. Everyone you love
will be dead,
or you will be dead
and none of that will matter then,
the lack
or the beauty. You will ask,

what was it about your generation
that only faggots
or the friends of faggots
knew what it was like to watch everyone they loved
die off, just like that.
Such poets, those poets
sucking one another off
in the food courts, and the dog parks, and the dance clubs.
Such poets, those young faggots
who lived.

It's more like that familiar wish
        to become a man when you are, in fact, a tributary.

Like the desire to have a body, never having had one.

Envision a room, live there for years/ live there for years.
        Get to know your fingers/ your fingers will get to know you.

Think, *Good. Someone knows me.*
        Do some math on a magazine cover. If you think,

*I was never any good but this is ridiculous now you're not working
in a factory a coffee shop a greenhouse you au pair-pornographic-*

actress-packer-shipper-receiver, for chrissakes don't marry

that man. Ten thousand days is a lot to have to forget… so go back.
The prairie may be wide and quiet. Doctors may shave your head

to make it easier for a needle to locate your brain. They may place
you in an oblong or opaque plastic bassinet or chamber to protect

70

you/not you from yourself/not yourself,

but just go.

No. Not whatever. Girl, you get yourself a roll of quarters. You eat the kosher meal.

The hair between your legs will seem familiar, if you touch it.

What's not to like she's got time for this
is a picture of you had better run take a Tylenol
an Aspirin an Advil or some other branded pain
killer please she's pleased to be here thankyou
thankyou thankyou and now she'll take a bow.
If you don't mind over matter well nothing really
matters anyway she's a freakish weather always gets
her downtown the lesbian community is eating itself
out of existence eventually everyone will have
an STD so what's the difference anyway. Classic
interlocutory parenthetical aside, (I say whoa there,
friend, unless you've got your key I just can't let
you in). Look, eventually, language became a get
over it under it couldn't so deep she get around
she wall it so wide. I'm [frustrated], she replied
sardonically. Kindled a fire with the delicate
hairs of a coconut husk, learned to blow in such
a way as to ignite only what needed ignition.

PIG IRON

No need to call on you. No need to invoke
what hunkers in the landfill. What makes
its mark in this epoch and the next? Dumbbell,
engine block. You leave your mark while all things fall
about you. Pressmen press your teeth into
what must become alluvium. Oh well,
for a time you've been out-of-date, corporeal
in the basements of the universities—
forgotten, forgotten, you wait for one big shake
to bring you to a head. Dumb material,
man-made metal thing. What did we make
when we thought that we made you? A handprint.
Something like a painting on a wall.
We were here, we said. You never left at all.

AT ROBERTS CREEK

Two swimmers, boys still, plunge into the sea.
Shrieks escape their lips. Who is that boy
ahead, and the one behind? You can see
that one is tentative while the other's joy
is to swim just a little too far from the shore.
I can see them from the cabin where I sit
writing this. I'm thirty-two. It's September.
What's important? His lime-green shorts
or his slender legs, like a girl's, kicking under him?
I don't know what's ahead any more
than they do. It's appalling, how far they've swum
while I sit here, helpless. I can't look anymore.
We've everything ahead, or nothing. Both are right.
The boys have drifted; now they're out of sight.

The history of Ukraine and of Ukrainians in Canada is fraught with tragedy, warfare, ethnic conflicts, racism, anti-Semitism, political intrigue, ecological disasters. There are stories of great bravery and bloodthirsty conquests, esoteric practices, and strange, strange rituals. It's a history that goes back thousands of years and begins somewhere on horseback on the Pontic steppe, guzzling blood from the skulls of its enemies. Dig deep enough through the midden and you'll hit burial chambers the size, shape and vintage of Egyptian pyramids. Cross the Atlantic and you see it through the barbed wire of internment camps in what is now Canada's national parks system.

By now, it is impossible to encapsulate all that is Ukrainian. It is an ethnicity that is, by its very nature, fractured, diasporic, transient; there is no one definition of what it is to be Ukrainian. It's not a new story, nor an unknown one, but there are over one million persons who claim Ukrainian heritage living in Canada today, and I suspect many of them, particularly people of my generation, are unaware of some basic history about both the Old Country and the New.

I can say this because I was one of them. We are cultural insiders and outsiders: inside, because our experiences have been drawn from a distinct, albeit particularly dispersed, cultural milieu within Canada, and outside because we have little or no direct experience of life in

Ukraine. Effectively, to locate the place from which I could write this text required that I locate my self, my gaze, my story.

Somewhere, you hear a choir singing the Ukrainian Orthodox liturgy. What are they singing? You can't quite catch it. It's thanksgiving. It's memory. Eat this bread. Pour this wax. Walk this city. Board this train. It's getting us somewhere.

–Elizabeth Bachinsky, Vancouver, BC

AUUC = Association of United Ukrainian Canadians

Kulak = From the Russian. Derogatory, meaning "tight-fisted." Kulaks were considered a wealthy class of farmers who resisted Stalin's plans for collectivization. In 1929, Stalin announced the "liquidation of the kulaks as a class." These farmers were persecuted through a process of political repression called "dekulakization" that could, among other punishments, include arrest, eviction, imprisonment, starvation and death.

The information in "The Bread Basket of Europe" was gathered from video footage on YouTube of interviews with survivors of the 1932–33 famine in Ukraine, Holodomor (sometimes known as "murder by hunger"), in which millions of people living in Eastern Ukraine were forcibly starved to death after having resisted Stalin's program of collectivization. The number of people reported to have perished in the famine ranges from 2.2 to 10 million. The heads of state, governments or parliaments of countries including Ukraine, Canada, Brazil, Georgia, Hungary, Moldova, Poland and the United States consider the famine an act of genocide.

The incantations found throughout this text are from Rena Jeanne Hanchuk's *The Word and Wax: A Medical Folk Ritual Among Ukrainians in Alberta.* They are reprinted here with the permission of CIUS Publications. Hanchuk writes: "During the wax ceremony (also known as 'the pouring forth of fear'), a patient who comes to a healer for help is seated in a chair. A bowl is filled with cold water, and a lump of wax is melted. The healer engages in conversation and asks the patient for his or her symptoms. An incantation is uttered, and the wax is poured into the water over the head of the patient.

The solidified wax is taken from the water and turned over and its shapes are interpreted. This process is typically repeated three times... The wax ceremony was important at the time of immigration and in the years that immediately followed. It nullified fear, nervousness, sleeplessness, and restlessness, social and psychological disorders that occurred among people who had emigrated to a strange and foreign land."

"The Wax Ceremony" draws on a number of print and online research materials. Those interested in a complete bibliography may contact the author through the press. Texts of particular significance to "The Wax Ceremony" include Bohdan Kordan and Peter Melnycky's *In the Shadow of the Rockies*; Bill Waiser's *Park Prisoners*; Orest Martynowych's *Ukrainians in Canada*; Helen Potrebenko's *No Streets of Gold* and the NFB film *Freedom Had a Price*.

"On the Day We Were Married" was inspired by the Hutzul marriage ceremony depicted in Sergei Parajanov's 1968 film *Shadows of Our Forgotten Ancestors*.

"God of Mechanical Accidents" and "Evolution of the Species" were written in response to Paul Fusco's photo essay, *Chernobyl Legacy*, which shows images of children living in the children's cancer hospital in Minsk, Belarus. The essay can be viewed online at: inmotion.magnumphotos.com/essays/chernobyl. aspx

A number of titles in this book (including the title of this book) were borrowed from a found list of gods and goddesses in David Byrne's book *Strange Ritual*.

ACKNOWLEDGEMENTS

"Morning Star" and "Goddess of Anthropomorphism" *Bei Mei Feng* (China)

"Goddess of Safe Travel," "Letter to my Sister," "To Ukraine," "Goddess of Chance Encounters" and "Ten Thousand Days" *ARC* Magazine

"Int. Back of Police Car. Night" and "Pig Iron" *This Magazine*

"Pig Iron" *The London Magazine* (UK)

"Gazers," "God of Chaos," God of Panic" and "God of Unfulfilled Longings" *fhole*

"Goddess of Missed Connections," "God of Mechanical Accidents" and "Tips on Performing from My Mother" *Matrix*

"The Day We Were Married" appeared as "Strange Ritual" in *Bellingham Review* (US)

"Brother My Brother Let's See What You Got" *sub-TERRAIN*

"Goddess of Chance Encounters" appeared in David Zieroth's *Poetry Strand*

"Morning Star" appeared as a Broadside for the Caledonia Writers' Series, College of New Caledonia

"Letter to My Sister" appeared online at the request of Canadian Parliamentary Poet Laureate John Steffler

Thanks to Trish Kelly (Chornyj) for asking me how things were going in the homeland; Sam Pane who hiked with me through the site of the Castle Mountain internment; Allan MacInnis for taking me to the Cinematheque to see Parajanov; Jenny Kindred and the Poltava Dancers for the tour of the AUUC hall in Regina; Silas White for putting me on to Paul Fusco; the Centre for Ukrainian Studies at the University of Alberta for all the textbooks; and my parents, Peter & Catherine Bachinsky, who are always generous with their stories.

"Tips on Performing from my Mother" is for my mom who spent her youth dancing at the AUUC Hall in Regina. "Letter to my Sister" and "Goddess of Safe Travel" is for my sister (and muse) Christine Bachinsky; "Hearsay in the Valley of Condominiums" is for Sachiko Murakami; "On the Day We Were Married" and "Morning Star" is for my husband Blake Smith; "God of Missed Connections" is for Matt Rader; "Young Faggots" is for Michael V. Smith and Peter Dubé.

Colin Bernhardt, Darren Bifford, Mary Dalton, Lee Gulyas, Rachel Lebowitz, Meredith Quartermain, Matt Rader, John Steffler, Silas White and Michelle Winegar—all helped shape this book. Particular thanks to Don McKay who edited much of this text with me at Banff. Thanks also to Sharon Brown & Andreas Schroeder, Amber Dawn, Jan & Crispin Elsted, Meredith & Peter Quartermain, and Anik See who opened their homes to me and offered me space to finish the work. Thank you.